NEW ZEALAND'S
WILD PLACES

NEW ZEALAND'S
WILD PLACES

CRAIG POTTON

craig potton publishing

NEW ZEALAND'S WILD PLACES

Maud Moreland came to New Zealand from England in the early 1900s to join her brother, the Reverend CH Moreland, who was then the principal of Christ's College in Christchurch.

In 1906 she and her brother undertook a remarkable five-week trip on horseback, from Christ-church over Arthur's Pass, down through South Westland, over Haast Pass and then home to Canterbury. Her account of the trip was subsequently published in a book Through South Westland, *from which the following extracts have been taken.*

They have been selected as an introduction to New Zealand's Wild Places *because they so eloquently capture the sense of wonder and delight that can be had from encountering New Zealand's natural world. Though over 100 years have passed since Maud Moreland completed her journey, these wild places are still to be found in New Zealand, and are still just as extraordinary. It is my hope that* New Zealand's Wild Places *can serve as a reminder of, and an inspiration for your own encounters with the wild places of our country.*

Craig Potton

Out of the town and along the dusty white road lined with trim houses, and gardens aglow with colour: on to country roads less dusty and with fewer and fewer houses, we rode forth one morning. It was six o'clock. The road-side herbage was drenched with dew. A grey-blue haze lay all over the wide Canterbury plains which seemed to stretch away to the farthest horizon, tall gum trees and fir plantations round the homesteads breaking the monotony of their flatness. Everywhere the crops were ripening to harvest; another week's sunshine and the wheatfields that waved all golden now would be cut. Fruit ripened in the orchards, and summer was at its height.

It was a blue day. All objects, near and far, were tinged with blue under the New Zealand sky, and as the sun got hotter, everything shimmered and trembled in the heat.

We breakfasted at a wayside inn, and rode on again, and when it grew unbearably hot we sought shelter at a little sun-baked place called Kirwee: just a few houses beside the inn, and a cabin of a railway station alongside the road—for railways and roads share the same wide tracks in the plains. Here we dawdled away the mid-day hours till teatime, and then as a little breeze sprang up we started to finish the forty-two miles to Mt. Torlesse.

The mountains had come into sight now. At first blue and featureless, then blacker and browner, the deeper valleys like splashes of purple. The first sight of their snowy tops made one forget the plains and the dusty road; our spirits rose, and we cantered fast along the wide, grassy margin. But we had lingered too long, and as we rode over an endlessly straight stretch, marked by clumps of black fir trees at regular intervals, the sudden-falling dusk came about us. The plain spread like a tawny sea to the foot-hills pushing out their purple headlands in cape and promontory:

> Darkly, like an armèd host
> Seen afar against the blue
> Rise the hills, and yellow-grey
> Sleeps the plain in cove and bay,
> Like a shining sea that dreams
> Round a silent coast.

Beyond lay a dead-white wall—a ghostly barrier of snow—between two purple ranges. All nearer objects became black and indistinct. Suddenly, behind the dead-white wall an orange light grew up, palpitating up and up past the zenith, till the night clouds overhead blazed out in gold and orange as it caught their edges. We watched it spread from bank to bank. Then came another change. The gold turned rosy red, then crimson, deeper and deeper, till all the clouds were blood-red, and we rode on in a darkening world, our eyes fixed on the glory above. It passed as suddenly as it came, and nought was left but a clear green streak of sky above the snow to show whence the glory had come; and then suddenly we realized it was dark, that we were tired, and the night grown chilly, and if we meant to arrive in any decent time that night, we must bestir ourselves. There were still seven miles to do, but we were sure of our welcome, no matter at what untimely hour we arrived. At last in the dusk we rode up to the hospitable door, and the master of Mt. Torlesse met us with a hearty greeting and bustled off the horses… After a day's rest we were rattled up betimes, and by four a.m. the Master of Torlesse was supplying our wants with hot coffee, and lecturing us on straps and the proper rolling up of our kit; and then rode with us the first three or four miles, to put us on our way. The Torlesse range lay grey and lifeless beyond the green paddocks and the crops round the homestead, and as we got among the stony hills the mist rolled down, alternating with bursts of sunshine. Everywhere stony rivers ran at the bottom of dreary valleys, with drearier hills rising up to stonier mountains, none over 6,000 feet, and all desolate. And when the afternoon came on, the rain came too, and we rode with heads down against a tearing south-west storm, that deluged us with sheets of water. Those were forty-four long miles…

But all things come to an end, and we saw the welcome end-gable of the Bealey Hotel on a rise above us…

We made up our minds to go on next day, and, fortunately for us, the weather proved fine.

We crossed the Waimakariri in safety, getting a beautiful view of snow mountains and glaciers at the head of the wide valley—a couple of miles, perhaps, across…

Once across, we rode up the Bealey. The gorge wound among steep mountains clothed in great part with the southern beech; waterfalls were frequent, and fine views of snow-capped ranges. Then we got to the divide called Arthur's Pass where are three small tarns lying on a mass of old moraine, which seems to fill the space between two parallel ranges. From one side of this the waters flow east, and from the other west. All this alpine meadow was beautiful with flowers: giant celmisias with satiny-white petals like enormous daisies, mingled with snow-white gentians, and the wonder of the Alps—the mountain lily [*Ranunculus lyallii*]. It is a pure white kingcup with golden centre, the leaves as large as saucers, and often the flowers are two or three inches across. As usual in the New Zealand mountains, most flowers were white. The plants here are specially interesting, because of the meeting of outliers from east and west. To a very large extent the western species do not grow on the east, except in certain places such as the Kaikouras, where the forest is very like a western forest. Farther south still, tree-ferns and pines occur; but, speaking broadly, the ranges on the east have beech forest, while the west has pine forest and a sub-tropical flora of its own.

The road zig-zagged in loops down a steep descent above a torrent. Bare, forbidding rocks and screens of loose stones ran up on one side, and presently we arrived at a place where they had all run down in a terrific rock-slide. The road was gone. A forlorn coach and one or two buggies had been abandoned there, but already a narrow track was scratched across the face of the débris. We led the horses over the sliding mass, and gained the undamaged road beyond. The road-menders told us of the violence of yesterday's storm which had wrecked the road, snapping off great forest trees, and strewing the track with wreckage. When we arrived at the Otira we found matters were in an even more congested state than at the Bealey. And still the people arrived! Not a bed or a towel was to be had, and at least sixty had slept there that night!

That was a glorious morning when we set out. The more sombre eastern colouring had given place to vivid greens; pine forest and ferns took the place of beech; above the gorge the snow peaks gleamed pure and sharp against the intense blue of the sky: it was enough to make the heart rejoice. And very joyous we were, as we rode down that sun-flecked woodland way, where the pinky track before us lay all mottled and barred with violet shadows. Bend after bend caught the morning sun as it poured a flood of golden light on tree-fern and unfamiliar foliage. Sometimes between the trees one caught sight of a snowy summit with mauve shadows on the snow, at the end of a purplish-blue vista. It was a fairyland of light and shade on dancing leaves, and on one side the river kept us company all the way: now swift and silent, eddying in blue-green streams, now tumbling over rocks in snowy foam.

Later I saw grander and more beautiful places, but the Otira taught me to love the road, wandering on and on beneath the trees, with its play of light and shade, its mystery and silence. The forest spoke then in an unknown tongue, but it was then I first heard its voice.

… We strolled away in the afternoon to see Lake Ianthe, being told it was but three-and-a-half miles off; but it seemed nearer five. At any rate it was well worth the walk. The road wound down to it through magnificent forest, where the tree-ferns expanded glorious fronds fifteen or twenty feet long, and everywhere grew a wealth of exquisite greenery. Strange new forms—new at least to our eyes—constantly attracted the attention. What the forest lacks in brilliancy of flowers, it gains in its wonderful variety of form. Except the ratas and a red honeysuckle, most of the flowers are white, or green and inconspicuous; but their perfumes are there, and every shade of green and gold and brown. Between the tall shafts of the trees we caught glimpses of a shining water, and we made our way to the shore and sat there entranced. The reflections were perfect: every leaf and twig, mountain summit, and sunset cloud lay there, as in a great looking-glass.

The snows of the distant Alps were flushing rosy-pink above the dark hills, clothed always to their tops with trees. And as we sat and watched, the water at our feet became golden with the reflection of the rosy cloudlets floating in it. Colours like the inside of a pearl-shell blended, and faded, and the evening mists crept over all, and we turned back down the darkening forest aisles. And as we went, the moonlight laid black bars across the road, and touched the giant ferns with silver, and every sound was hushed…

… From this place, named the Forks, we had a choice of ways—either to continue to the coast, visiting Okarito on its lagoon—one of the last nesting-places in the South Island of the white crane [or rather heron (*Herodias timoriensis*)]—or to turn inland along the Southern Alps. The road leads by Mapourika, most beautiful perhaps of New Zealand lakes, lying below the jagged peaks of the Minarets. Beyond, the great Franz Josef glacier winds down from those homeless wastes of ice and snow, where the Minarets and Mount Dela Bêche rear up like islands from the white expanse of the Tasman and adjoining glaciers. From their summits one looks, on the one hand across the eastern plains, and on the other over this green Western land of streams and forests, as Moses looked from Pisgah. Verily it is a Promised Land, but as yet the inheritance has not been wholly entered upon.

Mapourika is beautiful at all times in that wonderful setting of forest and mountain, but when the sunset flush on the peaks above is mirrored in the windless lake, and every tree and fern springs from its own double along the shore, I think it comes very near being Paradise…

The bad weather had spent itself, and as we got ready early next morning, a cloudless sky above the snow-peaks betokened a glorious day. Good-byes were said, and we fared forth once more down the Main South Road. It made a brave show with wide, cleared margins for a couple of miles or so, then deserted us in a river-bed, and when we picked it up again, it had become a pack track. This very soon dwindled to a narrow footpath, winding into the heart of the hills. The sun slanted down through the great trees over head:

> Their forest raiment . . . . from crown to feet
>   that clothed them royally,
> Shielding their mysteries from the glare of day.

Here, we were in a world untouched by man—save for that narrow, winding track—where the very birds seemed scarce to heed our presence, and the big bush-pigeons sat and looked at us from the miro trees—too lazy to fly away. The very loneliness but added to the wondrous, mysterious charm of this forest world. On and on we rode in the dewy freshness: round steep mountain flanks, up deep gorges, along rock-cut ledges where the yellow sunshine lay bright and warm on the rocky way, catching at times vistas of high mountains towering above us, shrouded always in impenetrable bush—it was, above all things, a forest ride. Always there was the crowding undergrowth beneath—that riot of green-life, of forms strange to our eyes, beautiful in their infinite variety. And everywhere were ferns. Who shall tell of the exquisite beauty of that fernery? They seemed to grow in colonies, sometimes of one kind, sometimes of another; and every fallen mossy trunk was covered with delicate hymenophyllums, like green lace. They climbed along the living branches, they draped the brown stems of the tree-ferns from base to crown—there they live and die uncared for, generation after generation, perfect in their beauty …

I had entered the promised land. I had seen a world as it was before man came there; in after years it would never be quite the same again. For if I went back to it, I might not find the Fairy Land of my dreams. The forest world must give place before the fire and the axe, but the memory of it, as I saw it in my brief sojourn, can never pass away.

So, as the sun sank behind the purple barrier of the western mountains, out-lining their edges in gold: and their long shadows stretched across the plain … I said, Farewell.

Maud Moreland

WILD COASTS

Because New Zealand has a complex geology and consists of two large, narrow islands, plus a host of smaller ones, its highly convoluted coastline is both exceptionally long and wonderfully varied. Just about every type of coastal geomorphology can be found, from fiords, sunken valleys and estuaries to sand spits, huge dune systems and quiet coastal coves and beaches. No place on the land is more than 130 kilometres from the ocean. And while most people live in cities beside the sea and travel to coastal holiday destinations, much of New Zealand's coast remains remote and pristine – nowhere more so than in South Westland and Fiordland in the South Island. Here, the primeval forests and wetlands stretch untouched from the mountains right to the ocean's edge.

To take in the full immensity and sweep of these extraordinary vistas, it is necessary to gain some elevation on a hill or coastal bluff. Two times of the day yield exquisite light for photography on these wild coasts – early morning when the sun climbs above the Southern Alps in the east, and the lingering twilight when the sun's rays streak out from beyond the horizon of the wind-tossed Tasman Sea in the west.

ABOVE Sea cliffs on Chalky Island, on the southwest coast of Fiordland National Park
OVERLEAF Mitre Peak reflected in the waters of Milford Sound on a winter morning, Fiordland National Park

Aerial view over Breaksea Sound, Fiordland National Park

Gog, one of the Fraser Peaks, Rakiura National Park, Stewart Island

West Ruggedy Beach, Rakiura National Park, Stewart Island

Tautuku Bay on the Catlins Coast, Southland

Black Head on the Otago Peninsula

Heretaniwha Point and Ohinemaka Beach in the evening, South Westland

Sunset at Ohinemaka Beach, South Westland

Granitic sand beach near Karamea, North Westland

Blowhole in the Pancake Rocks at Punakaiki, Paparoa National Park

ABOVE AND RIGHT Sea cliffs on the Truman Track, Paparoa National Park

Evening, Golden Bay

Moonrise, Golden Bay

Sand ripples at Awaroa Inlet, Abel Tasman National Park

Tide ripples over sand flats at Pakawau, Golden Bay

The Archway Islands off Wharariki Beach, Golden Bay

Rock formations at low tide on Wharariki Beach, Golden Bay

Sunrise on the Kaikoura coast and the Seaward Kaikoura Range, Marlborough

Sunset over Kapiti Island, from the coast north of Wellington

Sunrise at Awaroa Inlet, Abel Tasman National Park

The North Taranaki coast at Tongaporutu, with Mt Taranaki in the distance
OVERLEAF Pohutukawa flowering at Wainui Beach, near Gisborne

Coastal forest near Tutukaka, Northland

Volcanic ash deposits on White Island, Bay of Plenty

Sunrise on the Hauraki Gulf, looking east from Little Barrier Island (Hauturu)

Boulder Beach on Little Barrier Island (Hauturu), Hauraki Gulf

Rangitoto Island at sunrise, seen from Auckland's North Shore

Colony of Australasian gannets at Muriwai, Auckland

Looking south along Ninety Mile Beach, Northland

Cape Reinga, at the northwesternmost tip of the North Island

Sand dunes near Parengarenga Harbour, Northland

Sand dunes and exposed rocks in Te Paki Recreation Reserve, Northland

WILD FORESTS

New Zealand's forests began their evolution on an ancient southern hemisphere supercontinent called Gondwanaland. A proto-New Zealand landscape split apart from its Antarctic and Australian base 80 million years ago, with the result that many of today's conifers and podocarps are close ancestors of the so-called 'dinosaur' forests. The superabundance of ferns, lianes and mosses contribute to this legacy. This was an era before browsing mammals became dominant, and so the forests evolved in the absence of mammals and became populated with an array of endemic birds and insects that fill the niche of mammals in other lands. New Zealand's flora was also slow to speciate into flowering plants. Even the beech forests, which are predominant throughout much of the mountains and regions with poorer soils, have only diminutive flowers. Because few species in New Zealand are deciduous, forests are overwhelmingly green and beautifully complex in structure.

To photograph them one must seek out days of flat light with cloud cover or misty rain, as that is when reflection off the leaves is reduced and the colour saturation is sufficient to distinguish between the subtle variations of green. Before the arrival of humans, New Zealand was essentially a forested land and it is the remnants that remain which most distinguish it from other lands. It is to these remnants, some of which are actually still huge wildernesses, that I often return to be among the living green of New Zealand's forests.

Evening light on the rimu forest at Bruce Bay, South Westland

The kauri tree *Te Matua Ngahere* in Waipoua Forest, Northland

Tane Mahuta, New Zealand's largest living kauri tree, Waipoua Forest, Northland

The distinctive peeling bark of mountain cedar, or pahautea, Tongariro National Park

A grove of nikau palms on the Kermadec Islands, 1000 kilometres northeast of the North Island

Ferns and beech forest, Whirinaki Forest Park, Central North Island

Beech forest interior, Whirinaki Forest Park, Central North Island

Tree fern and beech trunks near Lake Waikareiti, Te Urewera National Park

Kahikatea trees in Arahaki Lagoon, Whirinaki Forest Park, Central North Island

Silver beech trees in mist on the Huiarau Range, Te Urewera National Park

Northern rata in flower, Golden Bay

Kahikatea forest on the shore of Lake Wahapo, South Westland

Kahikatea trees growing beside Lake Mapourika, Westland/Tai Poutini National Park

Forest of red and mountain beech in the West Sabine Valley, Nelson Lakes National Park

Moss-covered forest floor near the Hope Arm of Lake Manapouri, Fiordland National Park

Beech tree in snow, Aoraki/Mount Cook National Park

ABOVE Winter snowfall on beech forest at Flora Saddle, Kahurangi National Park
OVERLEAF The Southern Alps above lowland podocarp forest at Okarito, Westland/Tai Poutini National Park

Tree ferns in kamahi forest on the Minnehaha Walk, Fox Glacier, Westland/Tai Poutini National Park

Mosses and ferns on the trunk of a matai tree in the Oparara Basin, Kahurangi National Park

Alpine beech forest on the Kepler Track, Fiordland National Park

Beech trees beside Blue Lake, Nelson Lakes National Park

Rainforest interior, Fiordland National Park

Archeria traversii on the Hump Ridge Track, Southland

Mixed beech forest in the Clinton Valley on the Milford Track, Fiordland National Park

Hard beech trunk in rainforest near the North West Arm of Lake Te Anau, Fiordland National Park

WILD MOUNTAINS

The mountains of New Zealand are our most dramatic landforms. From the imposingly steep and dark diorite and granite of Fiordland to the shattered schist and greywacke of the Southern Alps and the majestic volcanic peaks of the Central North Island, New Zealand has a vast array of mountainous landscapes for such small islands. This diversity has created a wide range of habitats for flora and fauna, resulting in one of the highest rates of endemism in the world.

Although some mountains consist of old rocky formations, the ranges are, along with the coast, our youngest landforms; the Southern Alps having been thrust up in the last 10 million years along the fracture lines of one of the world's largest fault systems – the Alpine Fault. However, their rapid uplift is almost equalled by rampant erosion through heavy rain and, in the recent past, the weight and movement of huge glacial ice sheets during the ice ages.

To both Māori and Pakeha, mountains are the source of myths and the setting for heroic stories of Gods and men. One of the photographic methods I use to capture their obdurate presence and power is to line them up from directly in front, thus making them appear to come toward the viewer. Alternatively, I get high above them in a helicopter to reveal the never-ending vistas of thousands of mountain peaks shining above the clouds in the early morning or late evening light.

The Sheila Face of Aoraki/Mt Cook (3754 m), with Mt Hicks to the left, Aoraki/Mount Cook National Park

The granite domes of Gog (foreground) and Magog, Fraser Peaks, Rakiura National Park, Stewart Island

Granite boulders in the Fraser Peaks, Rakiura National Park, Stewart Island

Aerial view over the Heath Mountains, Fiordland National Park

Sunset on the Townley and Wall mountain ranges, Fiordland National Park

Mt Aspiring/Tititea (3033 m) and the Bonar Glacier from the southwest, Mount Aspiring National Park

Cloud-filled valleys in the Townley Mountains, Fiordland National Park

Sunset on the western face of Mt Aspiring/Tititea, Mount Aspiring National Park

Mt Dechen (2643 m) on the Hooker Range, Hooker/Landsborough Wilderness Area, South Westland

Evening light catches a peak on The Remarkables, Central Otago

The Sheila Face of Aoraki/Mt Cook, looking northwest to Mt Tasman, Aoraki/Mount Cook National Park

Erosion-resistant schist tors on the broad summit of the Old Man Range, Central Otago

<small>ABOVE</small> Clay cliffs near Omarama in the Mackenzie Country, Canterbury
<small>OVERLEAF</small> Tussock grassland at Lindis Pass, Otago

The East Face of Aoraki/Mt Cook and the Grand Plateau, Aoraki/Mount Cook National Park

ABOVE Mt Tasman (3491 m) from the northeast, Aoraki/Mount Cook National Park
OVERLEAF Speargrass in the Hooker Valley, with Aoraki/Mt Cook beyond, Aoraki/Mount Cook National Park

The Minarets (3040 m) from the Tasman Glacier, Aoraki/Mount Cook National Park

Mt Green and Mt Walter above the Tasman Glacier, Aoraki/Mount Cook National Park

Snowfields and peaks below the western flanks of Mt Tasman (centre), Westland/Tai Poutini National Park

Cloud to the west of Mt Sefton (3151 m) and the Main Divide, Aoraki/Mount Cook National Park

The source of the Waiho River at Franz Josef Glacier, Westland/Tai Poutini National Park

ABOVE Franz Josef Glacier, Westland/Tai Poutini National Park
OVERLEAF The névé of the Fox Glacier, Westland/Tai Poutini National Park

Paschendale Ridge and the Albert Glacier above Fox Glacier (right), Westland/Tai Poutini National Park

Icefall on the Franz Josef Glacier, Westland/Tai Poutini National Park

Winter snow on Mt Una (2300 m), Nelson Lakes National Park

ABOVE A corniced ridgeline on Mt Una in the Spenser Mountains, Nelson Lakes National Park
OVERLEAF Mt Taranaki (2518 m) and Fanthams Peak, Egmont National Park

ABOVE AND RIGHT The 1996 eruption of Mt Ruapehu (2797 m), Tongariro National Park

Mt Ngauruhoe (2287 m) in winter from Mt Ruapehu, Tongariro National Park

Mt Ruapehu's crater lake after the 1995 eruption, Tongariro National Park

Red Crater and Blue Lake on the Tongariro Alpine Crossing, Tongariro National Park

The volcanic features of Mt Tarawera, near Rotorua, Central North Island

WILD RIVERS AND LAKES

Situated in the westerly wind belt of the world's largest ocean with high mountains to trap every drop of rain, New Zealand has a phenomenal freshwater world, which encompasses slow-moving glaciers, raging rivers, extensive lakes and quiet wetlands. The cycle always starts with water in a pristine state, but it is then subject to degradation from human usage and abuse. Thankfully however, many New Zealand rivers still run wild and free into lakes or the turbulent sea.

New Zealand's island isolation has created freshwater habitats that have evolved in their own way for upwards of 80 million years, so that the plants and animals found there are mostly endemic species. New Zealand has one of the last large populations of freshwater eels in the world, and many species of a unique fish type, the galaxiids.

Water is the most elusive medium to photograph in that, like the sky, it is almost impossible to convey a sense of depth. However, it is more reflective than the atmosphere, and in rivers it is constantly on the move. I don't deliberately seek to make the water surface silken in appearance; that is merely the side effect of a slow shutter speed to gain depth of field. I constantly return to our rivers and lakes as no two water shots are ever the same, even if the composition is – the subject is always on the move.

ABOVE Lake Hauroko, Fiordland National Park
OVERLEAF Blue Lake fills a volcanic crater on Mt Tongariro, Tongariro National Park

Te Whaiti Nui A Toi canyon in Whirinaki Forest Park, Central North Island

Korokoro Falls, near the Lake Waikaremoana Track, Te Urewera National Park

Pohutu Geyser in Whakarewarewa Thermal Reserve, Rotorua, Central North Island

Kowhai on the shores of Lake Taupo, Central North Island

The Waikato River above Huka Falls, Taupo, Central North Island

Waireinga/Bridal Veil Falls, Raglan, Waikato

Limestone formations in the Waitomo Caves, Waikato

ABOVE Champagne Pool, Waiotapu Thermal Area, Rotorua, Central North Island
OVERLEAF Winter snow above Lake Manapouri, Fiordland National Park

Moria Gate in the Oparara Basin, Kahurangi National Park

A waterfall on the Mangatini Stream, North Westland

Angelus Peak reflected in Lake Angelus, Nelson Lakes National Park

Beech forest beside the West Sabine River, Nelson Lakes National Park

Looking east over the Clarence River in winter, Marlborough

Tilted rock strata beside the Clarence River, Marlborough

Lake Hawea, Central Otago

Lake Tekapo at the northern edge of the Mackenzie Basin, Canterbury

Red tussock on the shores of Lake Alexandrina, Canterbury

Lake Pukaki with Aoraki/Mt Cook in the distance, Canterbury

Aoraki/Mt Cook beyond flats on the Tasman River, Aoraki/Mount Cook National Park

Aerial view over Mt Crichton and Lake Wakatipu, Otago

Sutherland Falls dropping from Lake Quill, Fiordland National Park

Giant Gate Falls on the Milford Track, Fiordland National Park

Morning mist at Lake Paringa, South Westland

ABOVE Norwest Lake, situated above Lake Manapouri, Fiordland National Park
OVERLEAF The Southern Alps beyond Lake Matheson, Westland/Tai Poutini National Park

Kahikatea and flax growing beside Lake Mapourika, Westland/Tai Poutini National Park

Water-worn limestone rock, Paparoa National Park

First published in 2013

Craig Potton Publishing, 98 Vickerman Street, PO Box 555, Nelson, New Zealand

www.craigpotton.co.nz

© Photography: Craig Potton

ISBN 978-1-927213-01-8

Printed in China by Midas Printing International Ltd